Postcards To Myself
A Journey of Self-Discovery

By GG RUSH

Postcards To Myself

A Journey of Self-Discovery

As You Wish Publishing, LLC

Connect@asyouwishpublishing.com

ISBN-13: 978-1-951131-40-1

Library of Congress Control Number: 2021923917

Printed in the United States of America.

Nothing in this book or any affiliations with this book is a substitute for medical or psychological help. If you need help please seek it.

"I am loyal and constant in my love of travel." —Elizabeth Gilbert

"Travel makes one modest. You get to see what a tiny place you occupy in the world." —Gustave Flaubert

"The world is a book, and those who do not travel read only one page." —St. Augustine

Table of Contents

"Traveling – it leaves you speechless, then it turns you into a storyteller." —Ibn Battuta

D on't be afraid. Take my hand, and let's board that airplane and jet off to some exotic places and see the world. Seven years ago, I decided to live my lifelong dream of seeing the world. Alone. Yes, ALONE. Why? Because I also needed to find my authentic self, and I didn't want to be burdened with filling the needs of anyone else for nine or ten days. You see, I am a caregiver. A single mom with elderly parents and a job that assigned me the role of Mother Hen to the staff. I set my sights on finally fulfilling a quest to travel. So I started thinking seriously about my week vacation from work. I wanted this, and I saw myself doing it. About a week later, I got an email: "Groupon Getaways." I opened it and discovered very affordable vacations with Groupon. Yes, it is true; the opportunity to travel to so many places included airfare, hotel, trains between cities, breakfast and some tours.

As I browsed the trips and itineraries, I realized this was a gift to myself that I could afford. I started asking people about their favorite places. I heard "Spain" from a few folks. There was an 8-day package to Spain. Three cities with hotels, trains and meals. That was my first trip. Bali, Iceland and

CHAPTER ONE

Italy followed. Africa came next but let's save that one for later.

Are Groupon deals good deals, and are the hotels ok or are they dives? These are the questions I get most often. My answer is I have never been disappointed. Based on the experiences of the people I meet who are also on a Groupon package during my adventures, there are no complaints.

I booked that trip to Spain four months before I went. Groupon sets you up with the travel agency that has the offer. They were accommodating and helpful. Yet, I was nervous for weeks. Had I made a mistake? When it came time to board that flight, would I chicken out? How would I manage to do this all by myself? My daughters were so supportive. My mother was so worried. My friends were astonished. I was scared. I bought a new suitcase and a backpack. I pulled out my much-neglected passport with one stamp to my niece's wedding in Jamaica. I boarded a flight from Raleigh to

DC and then DC to Paris. When the flight attendant brought a dinner menu, I naively asked the person next to me, "Do we pay for this dinner?" No, because you see on international flights, even in the cheap seats, they take good care of you. It's a long ride, and they want you to be content. As the flight came close to the end, breakfast was served. After a short layover in Paris, I flew on to Madrid and on that flight, the attendant brought around a basket of sandwiches.

I learn things on every trip, and I now consider myself a seasoned veteran traveler. At the end of this book, I will share with you my top tips for your journey. I hope that you will meet me at the departure gate and we will travel the world. Bon Voyage, and we are off to Spain!

Wanderlust (n): a strong desire for or impulse to wander or travel and explore the world.

CHAPTER TWO – SPAIN

"It's like a dream to come to Spain and stay for a couple of years and get somebody to teach me Spanish music." —Lenny Kravitz

Touch down Madrid-Barajas Adolfo Suarez Airport. I am alone in a foreign country. For the first time in my life. Paris France doesn't count since it was a very short layover at the airport. My passport was stamped in Paris, and I am slightly disappointed not to have it stamped in Madrid. Over the years, I will find that this happens when you travel through countries to your final destination.

I follow the other passengers since I have no idea where I am going. There is no customs. I am out in the arrival area and look for the driver I have booked with my Groupon. I see my name on a placard, and the driver greets me in English. Everyone speaks English as well as many other languages in Europe. I am delivered to my hotel via a Mercedes Benz coupe and am greeted enthusiastically at the desk. The local travel agent is waiting for me with my itinerary, train tickets and maps. She is very welcoming and gives me her cell number if I need anything. I get my room key and take my suitcase and backpack upstairs. The room is clean and comfortable, with a courtyard view. My worst fear was that it would be awful, but it isn't. It is quite pleasant!

I am exhausted, but it is early in the day in Spain. I must leave my room. I am afraid. What if I am mugged or molested? What if I get lost and can't speak more than high school Spanish? I pull out the travel agent's map of Madrid, where she has circled my hotel location. I see something familiar that my Spanish boss has recommended as a must-see. Plaza Mayor and Mercado San Miguel! Only a few blocks on the same street as my hotel! I'm in Madrid, and I must leave the safe space of my hotel room in order to actually experience this country. I tell the desk clerk I am going to explore and show her the map, and she actually takes note that I am alone, and I feel comfortable knowing she will watch for my return. This practice will become a habit from now on to make myself known to the front desk. I step outside the hotel entrance and feel momentarily overwhelmed by the rush of this city. I turn to the right and start putting one foot in front of the other. The sidewalk is cobbled in places, and as an inexperienced traveler, I have not worn the best walking shoes. Note to self: buy Band-aids. And good walking shoes.

I reach an arched area and enter Plaza Mayor. This is the main "square" in Madrid. There are many plazas throughout the city. Café's and artists, and street entertainers are everywhere. I stop at a fountain and read my guidebook. Shops are plentiful here, and above them are high-dollar apartments. What must it be like to live in such a place? I stroll around, looking at the artists at work. I stop in the Museo del Jamon. The Ham Museum. I browse the tourist shops noting the Flamenco Girl and Bullfighter magnets that I will bring home to friends. I follow my map and exit on the side of the plaza, and right in front of me is the Mercado San Miguel. I enter the crowded market, and my senses are overwhelmed with wines, cheeses, olives and, of course, ham. I buy a glass of red wine and some cheese and olives and sit in a crowded bistro area. After my tapas snack, I follow my route back to my hotel, pleased with myself for this adventure. Then I sleep.

The next day I have a reservation in the early evening at the world's oldest restaurant Sobrino de Botin. I pull out my map and see that it is around the corner from Mercado San Miguel, and I already know how to get there. But my first destination is the Royal Palace. I walk back to the Plaza Mayor and then the few blocks to the palace and wait in line for my ticket. The inside of the palace is opulent. Amazing furnishings and paintings by Goya, Caravaggio and other Spanish Masters. In the music room, I find a complete Stradivarius quintet of stringed instruments. The guide explains they are still played for special occasions. I love history and art and architecture, and I am humbled by what I have already seen in the course of my first real tour.

I venture back the same way I have come, and when I get to the Mercado, I round a street corner with cafés and buildings with flower boxes and stumble on Botin. I am very early for my reservation, but they are open, so I chance it. Besides, I am weary and hungry. They accommodate me in the downstairs dining room, and my table is precariously perched next to some stone stairs leading to the wine cellar. I am careful not to tip my chair and fall into the abyss. Botin is famous for suckling pigs, but I'm not ready to eat a baby pig. I order Sangria and the other famous dish, garlic soup. A British couple and their guide come next to my table to enter the ancient wine cellar. I smile at them, and the guide asks me if I would like to join them. Oh yes, please! We enter the cool, damp cellar, and the guide tells us that the cellar contains a passage that leads to an underground tunnel that connects to the palace and that the Royals of the past used it to travel incognito through the city. The guide offers to take a picture of me in front of some vintage wine bottles. For the first time, I realize that traveling alone can have some very special perks if you seize the opportunity.

The next morning I am off to the train station by taxi, and I find the driver is better at English than I am at Spanish, and I make it safely and pay the correct amount for the fare. The Madrid train station is a bit overwhelming, but I am now a little bolder, and I ask for directions. I board the train to Córdoba.

I have my Nook loaded with books, but I don't even take it out of my backpack. The bullet train gains speed, and I watch the passing of the city, which then turns more rural and then gives way to vineyards and olive groves. Towns dot the countryside, and all of them have a church at the center. Andalusia is a beautiful region. After a long journey, the train pulls into Córdoba station, which is much smaller than the vast Madrid station. Córdoba was once a Roman city and an Islamic center. Full of Moorish architecture and influences. I get a taxi, and off we go to my next hotel. We leave the city and enter a more residential area, and I am a bit confused, but the driver turns onto a side street lined with expensive-looking gated homes and a golf course. Groupon has booked me at a golf course resort! My room is lovely with Spanish tiled floors and a huge soaking tub in accented tiles.

Once again, I tell myself I must venture out since I only have one day and night here. The front desk clerk tells me the shuttle is already out but that if I walk to the end of the street, I can catch a bus to downtown. She helps me with figuring the fare. I wait at the bus stop with two women who are maids who work in the neighborhood. I point at the map and where I want to go, and they nod and smile, and when the bus arrives, they sit with me. When we reach downtown, they pull me up and point and gesture to walk in that direction. I leave my new friends, and with the help of my trusty map, I venture down many narrow alleyways twisting and turning; not sure I can retrace my path, I keep pushing forward. All at once, I emerge into a park and ahead is my intended destination. La Mezquita is an immense mosque built in 784 AD. After buying my ticket, I am glad to enter the mosque as the heat of the day has intensified.

Inside I am humbled by the beauty of the Byzantine mosaics and the 856 red and white arched columns of the main prayer room. The history doesn't end there, as inside the mosque is the Cathedral of Our Lady of the Assumption—a Catholic Cathedral INSIDE an Islamic Mosque. This, to me, is what religion should be about. There is a baptism going on, and I watch from the back of the cathedral. The Mezquita is filled with treasures. It remains one of the most interesting places I have been fortunate to see in person.

When I exit the mosque, I am greeted by the unnatural sight of a Subway restaurant. Surreal. It is extremely hot, and I hail a taxi as I am not up for those alleyways and the bus. When I return to the hotel, I take a cooling dip in the swimming pool and have a cold Sangria from the pool bar. I had dinner of roasted pork and rice sitting on the veranda.

The next morning I am off again on the train to the city of Sevilla. Once again the countryside passes by and gives way to the suburbs and city. Another taxi ride to my hotel, which is in the Triana District. The hotel is again lovely and in a shopping and residential area. I get my bearings and walk to Maria Luisa Park, which is similar to New York Central Park with ponds and statues and gardens. I follow a path and emerge at the Plaza de España. Built in 1928 for an Exposition, the plaza is a tiled masterpiece with a moat and bridges. Tiled alcoves of each province of Spain are represented. I sit for a while on the steps and take in the magnificent beauty of this place. A vendor is selling Spanish fans, and I buy several in rich colors. They now hang in my office at my workplace. I walk back to my hotel, stopping for tapas and a glass of wine at a café before retiring to my room. I should note here that for the first time, I witness the buildings and shops shuttering up for siesta time. Everything closes down for a heavy meal and a nap.

The next day proves to be magical. After a hotel breakfast of bread with the greenest olive oil I have ever seen, meats and cheeses and strong coffee, I am ready for my day. I cross the Triana Bridge and head toward the spires of the Cathedral. My first stop is the Real Alcázar, the Royal Palace of Sevilla. It is a wonder of tiles, fountains and the most beautiful gardens. It was the location shoot for the *Game Of Thrones* city of Dorne. I spent longer than planned wandering the gardens, sitting on cool stone benches and breathing in the fragrance of orange blossoms.

I cross the courtyard to the Cathedral and the Giralda Tower. I always find the most incredible art and artifacts in Cathedrals and places of worship. Sevilla Cathedral did not disappoint. Unfortunately, the Giralda Tower was closed for repairs, so I missed the fabulous view of the city that is bragged about. I had extra time on my walk back to the hotel, so I stopped at the Torre del Oro, the Tower of Gold on the river. On a whim, I bought a ticket for a boat tour and saw the city from the Guadalquivir River. After more tapas and Sangria, I took a much-needed nap.

During the time of year that I was in Sevilla, it stayed light late into the night. I grabbed a taxi and went to the Barrio Santa Cruz in search of Casa de la Guitarra. A guitar museum with a nightly Flamenco show. It turned out I didn't really need that cab, and the streets are so narrow he almost didn't make it. I could see the spires of the Cathedral and the tower, so I knew my way back. The show was so moving. Just one guitar player, a singer and a dancer. The dancer's polka dot gown was a traditional Flamenco style. I cried several times at the beauty of the performance.

Walking back that evening, I stopped four times at different cafés and sampled a tapas dish and Sangria. The last stop was at the foot of the bridge overlooking the river. What a delightful end to my visit.

The next day after a direct train trip, I was back in Madrid and my original hotel room. My last sightseeing day was spent at the Prado Art Museum with its world-class collection of masters. One more visit to the Mercado San Miguel for my dinner, and I was off to the airport and home. My first solo trip was a success, and I had been bitten by the travel bug!

"Any reasonable, sentient person who looks at Spain, comes to Spain, eats in Spain, drinks in Spain, they're going to fall in love. Otherwise, there's something deeply wrong with you. This is the dream of all the world."

—Anthony Bourdain

Gratitude Message:

I am grateful to myself. Taking a chance and stepping outside my comfort zone. Choosing Spain as my first adventure. Flamenco music and dance. Tapas and wine. Orange blossoms. The reverence of the Mosque and the Cathedral. A beautiful night in Sevilla. I am grateful for my bravery and fortitude in taking this chance. Thank you, Groupon. I give thanks for this experience.

CHAPTER THREE – BALI

"Bali is more than a place…it's a mood, it's magical. It's a tropical state of mind."
—Unknown

Where would I go next? I studied the Groupon Getaways offers. A cruise down the Volga sounded interesting. St. Petersburgh, Moscow and the Bolshoi Ballet. But there it was. Bali. A place I knew from one of my favorite books, *Eat Pray Love* by Elizabeth Gilbert. This was the place for me. The Groupon pictures showed a tranquil place with ancient temples and tropical beaches. I booked it.

It took 24 hours to get to Bali via Los Angeles and Taipei. The Taipei airport has spectacular themed gates. One filled with orchids from the Taipei Orchid Society. My gate was the Hello Kitty gate. From Taipei to Bali and back, I flew on the Hello Kitty plane. Everything was Hello Kitty, including the toilet paper. The flight attendants had retro-looking uniforms and beehive hairdos. They wore Hello Kitty aprons when serving. It was magical.

I arrived in Bali during Galungan, a celebration honoring ancestral spirits. Every home and business decorate bamboo structures of various sizes called Penjor. They line the streets and villages. They hold offerings and little boxes for their ancestral spirits to visit. I was really lucky to have gotten to see this beautiful celebration going on. Every morning small offerings are left outside every doorway. You have to watch your step. You also have to watch out for the scooters. They are the number one mode of transportation, and the Balinese people apparently have no fear when driving them. Sometimes entire families are riding on one scooter. Clinging to each other as they weave in and out of traffic. Once I even saw two men and a goat on one. Yes, seriously, a goat!

My first hotel was Ossotel in Seminyak, a popular beach community. This was the first time I tried to upgrade, and the concierge was very accommodating, putting me in a first-floor swim-up room exactly as pictured on the Groupon site! The rooms were cool and tiled with a huge walk-in shower with a rain showerhead which I had never used before.

On this particular trip, I didn't sign up for any group tours other than the one that would take us between hotels. It was very cheap in Bali, so I opted for a driver for two days. The first morning Ketut arrived in his minivan to take me out to see the country. He was very nice, and I immediately felt comfortable with him. We left the city and drove through villages, and Ketut explained about Galungan. He also explained that each region has a temple, each village has a temple, and each home has a small temple or shrine. Ketut took me to an ancient temple where the Hindu priest wrapped a colorful cloth skirt around my waist so I could enter. Ketut held my arm as we climbed the stone stairway. The beautiful carvings in the stone were a wonder to see. Ketut pointed to a tower that held a huge gong and explained how warnings or calls to gather were heard for miles. Ketut took my camera from me and snapped photos of me in my skirt in front of the temple.

Next, we traveled to Penglipuran Village, a model of a traditional Balinese village.

The pathways were lined with Penjor. It was an interesting glimpse of how the Balinese people live. I was growing very tired by then, jetlagged and drained. Ketut said we had one more stop that day, and I admit I dozed in the airconditioned comfort of the minivan. I awoke when we came to a stop and found myself at a very busy, very touristy-looking place. Ketut shielded me from the vendors trying to sell me trinkets. I was a little dazed, and Ketut pointed out the volcano in the distance. He sensed I was tired and a bit overwhelmed, and he guided me back to the minivan. But something caught my eye. Dogs. In cages being sold in the market. Oh no. I asked Ketut if they were for food, and he smiled and shook his head. On the ride back to Seminyak and the hotel Ketut taught me about the Kintamani, a uniquely Balinese dog breed. Very popular and very loved. Dogs are everywhere in Bali, roaming the streets and villages. And after my lesson, I began to notice the similarities in them.

I returned to the hotel tired but filled with so much culture and history. Ketut would pick me up again in the morning, and I headed straight to my swim-up room and took advantage of the pool and chaise lounge and a hand-delivered martini.

The typical hotel breakfast in Bali involves rice or noodles and eggs. And the freshest juice of papaya, mango and orange. Balinese coffee is world-famous and involves a small cat-like mammal called a civet. You might want to look that process up.

Ketut arrived and whisked me away to Tanah Lot temple, the most famous of the Balinese temples. Tanah Lot sits on a rock in the sea. Tourists are not allowed to actually enter the temple itself but can reach the grounds at low tide. Needless to say, the area is a tourist mecca and very crowded, but getting my picture taken at Tanah Lot was worth the crowds. There are lots of souvenir shops and places to eat as well. Ketut and I enjoyed an iced treat under a large shade tree.

Our next stop was a theatre where Ketut waited outside while I watched the Barong Dance Performance. The musicians sat on the floor, and the dancers and performers were on a large stone stage. Traditional Balinese dance and costumes are featured. Barong is the leader of good, and Rangda is the enemy. It was fascinating and beautiful.

We stopped at a Batik shop where I purchased some silk scarves and watched some ladies' batik handiwork. Then my time with Ketut came to an end, and we said farewell. Every now and then, after all these years, we still email from time to time.

I took a stroll on Seminyak beach and watched the world-famous surfers take on huge waves. Dogs roamed the beach in packs. I watched the gorgeous sunset and felt such peace from all I had seen in just two days. And I still had five more days.

I rode with some other Groupon tourists in a van to our next destination, the city of Ubud. On our way, we stopped at a silver shop. Bali is famous for silver. And I am particularly fond of dragonflies. This was no ordinary jewelry store. The outside was covered in ornate dragonflies! We first toured the silversmith shop and watched the artisans crafting intricate designs. Once we entered the enormous showroom, it was overwhelming. I purchased a silver dragonfly necklace that is my favorite piece of jewelry ever. I wear it almost daily.

Our driver took us to a family compound so we could see behind the walls of a Balinese home. There were a series of huts that were for cooking and living. Heritage is very important in Bali. The grandparents have a place, the parents a place and the children a place. The mother served us some delicious coconut rice that she was cooking in a large pot over a fire. The family showed us their garden, livestock and shrine. It was a fascinating opportunity for our group.

My next hotel was very different from the modern Ossatel. Every room was actually an individual hut. Mine was next to the hotel shrine. The grounds were gardens with a flowing stream running through with little bridges connecting pathways. Large golden fish swam, and lily pads floated serenely. It was very tranquil. The first morning, there was a short rain shower, and I sat on my little front porch and listened to the rain and the birds.

I had booked a spa treatment up in the mountains above the bustling city of Ubud, and the hotel driver took me on a hair-raising ride up the mountain in a modified golf cart. I saw large homes hanging cliffside as we whizzed along. I still can't believe that golf cart made it up that mountain, but we arrived at Karsa Spa. The spa grounds overlook rice patties and farmland. I had a half-day booked and was in for an amazing experience. The massage rooms are private but open air. A large stone tub with a reclining buddha watching over dominates the space. An open stone shower and massage table take up the rest of the space. The masseuse was a smiling Buddha-like lady, and she was excellent. After covering me in a coffee scrub, she filled the tub with water and flowers and gestured to the shower and the tub and left me alone. I sat in that tub for probably an hour, taking it all in and enjoying every second until she returned and took me to another smaller room for a facial. That was followed by a pedicure in an outdoor area where another guest dozed next to me and gently snored, causing the pedicure girls to giggle and wink at me. Karsa Spa was a splendid experience. The hotel driver returned, this time in an SUV, so my ride was less hair raising.

At dinner, I sat with two ladies who wanted to know all about the spa, but I really wanted to know about their day spent searching for the medicine man from *Eat, Pray, Love.* Sadly, I didn't tell them that I had seen something about his passing. They did see a medicine man, just not that one. We enjoyed chatting over wine and a Bali barbeque-type meal. What a wonderful day.

The next day, I stayed in and enjoyed the hotel grounds and pool. I sat in the open-air dining room, watching the traffic pass and the street dogs. I crossed the busy road, barely escaping a scooter disaster and did some shopping. Just some downtime on my own.

On my final day, I rode on the golf cart with a young couple going into town to explore. I was going to take in the Sacred Monkey Forest. The young couple had been the day before and told me to take the advice of not bringing food and watching my backpack. The monkeys are very curious and smart, and they will open your backpack and steal your sunglasses if given a chance!

I entered the Monkey Forest, clutching my backpack and guarding my sunglasses and my hat. The forest is huge, and yes, it is full of monkeys. Large monkeys. Mama monkeys with adorable baby monkeys. Monkey keepers in bright uniforms watching over the monkeys. Winding pathways, sculptures, and abundant foliage make it a real sanctuary in the heat of the day. Rounding a corner, I came upon one of the temples on the grounds. Hundreds of monkeys climbed the temple walls and roof.

I sat quietly and watched a Japanese family disobey the guidelines. The mother took some cookies from her bag and gave them to her slightly whiney children. Oops, not a good idea! Several monkeys surrounded the children and swiped their snacks! I shouldn't have been amused, but they weren't hurt, and well, they didn't listen.

I left the Monkey Forest and walked the streets of Ubud, stopping at the temple in the heart of the city. I considered walking back to the hotel when I ran into the young couple from earlier. They were so excited to have just spent an hour at a Cat Café. I had never heard of such a place, but now I know they are trendy, and I have seen them in other places in the world. We caught the golf cart back and shared a bottle of wine in the garden.

My last day in paradise. A typhoon was threatening Taipei and our worried group went to the airport wondering if we would beat it. The Hello Kitty plane got us to Taipei, and the very efficient Taipei airport staff was detouring passengers away from Immigration and Customs and getting us on board our flights very quickly. I avoided that Typhoon and returned safely, 24 hours later, home.

Bali was a very spiritual country. The people are poor but happy in their lives. Friendly and outgoing, and generous. I will never forget my journey and those monkeys.

"Religious ceremonies are of paramount importance in Bali: (an island, don't forget, with seven unpredictable volcanoes on it – you would pray, too." —Elizabeth Gilbert

Gratitude Message:

I am grateful to have met the gentle, happy spiritual people of Bali. The beauty of their island home is filled with sacred places and traditions. The welcoming love and kindness of the Balinese people were a lesson for me. The colorful batiks and the silly monkeys and the lifelong friendship of my driver companion for making me feel safe. I give thanks for this experience.

CHAPTER FOUR – ICELAND

"There is no more sagacious animal than the Icelandic horse. He is stopped by neither snow, nor storm, nor impassable roads, nor rocks, glaciers, or anything. He is courageous, sober and surefooted."
—Jules Verne

I am a student of Reiki, and I am an Empath. I feel the energy around me when I attune to it. Iceland is ground zero for energy. During my time there, I will feel slightly unsettled at first, not understanding what it is that I feel coming up through my feet and coursing through my body, mind and spirit. It is the earth's energy. Real and pure and natural. Unfiltered even through the thick soles of my hiking boots. After the first day, I will understand this strong current of natural energy. And not just the elements of volcanic energy but of the glacier-pure water and the fresh air. And the spirits of the legendary Hidden People. The spirit of the tiny horses. The power of the geysers. Standing in my bare feet in the hotel room, gazing at the snow-capped mountains in the distance across the bay, I feel something flowing. I have never been anywhere before, or since, that I felt this close to Mother Earth.

Iceland: The land of Fire and Ice. Volcanos and Glaciers. I arrive via Toronto. A light rain falls, and the sky is gray. The tour van is warm and quiet. A group of weary travelers ready to see this amazing country. Our guide Anna tells us she is a school teacher and her English is perfect. She explains that English is required in school for all students. The airport is about 30 miles from the city of Reykjavik, which will be my home for the next week. This getaway has only one hotel stay, and I have booked two days of group tours with Anna.

The landscape on the ride from the airport is strange, almost lunar looking since we are driving through a lava field. We arrive in the city and make three stops at different hotels, and Anna explains that because it is very early in the morning, we will not be able to check-in immediately, but we can store our luggage and have breakfast. She also explains that the water is safe to drink directly from the tap because it comes from the glaciers. So begins my addiction to Icelandic water, which by the way, you can order by the case from Amazon.

My hotel is Hotel Cabin, located a block from the waterfront. Breakfast every morning is the same. Meats, cheeses, breads and porridge. We fill our water bottles from pitchers that the dining room staff keeps filled for just this purpose. Anna and our driver Lars have returned with the folks who were dropped at their hotels before us. Anna explains we will be taking in some sights since we have no rooms yet.

Our first stop is the towering Hallgrimskirkja church. Try pronouncing that! There will be many challenging names in the days ahead. The church dominates the center of the city. There has been a service going on since we have arrived on a Sunday morning. This is a Lutheran church, and I am familiar with the service as I was raised Lutheran. An enormous pipe organ is a focal point. The music being played is beautiful. Anna ushers us silently outside and says we don't have time to go to the top of the tower, but we should all find an opportunity to return as the 360-degree views are breathtaking. She points out the statue of Leif Erikson in the courtyard, and the statue was a gift from the United States.

We next arrive at Perlan, a futuristic glass dome that houses a museum, restaurant and observation deck. Out on the observation deck, I encounter my first blast of Icelandic wind. I have more of that in store. We all snap the obligatory photo and trundle back to the warm van. Everyone is very jet-lagged.

The Northern Light Experience is very much anticipated as we will be inside for an hour. I have booked my trip at a time when I will not be experiencing the natural Northern Lights due to the long daylight hours this time of year. Poor planning on my part. The synthetic show makes me wish I was able to see this phenomenon. Some group members, including me, struggle to stay awake in the darkened theatre room, but the show is magnificent.

On our return trip to the hotels, we briefly stop at the Harpa Concert Hall, a magnificent honeycomb glass building on the waterfront. Reykjavik is a city of old classic buildings and modern architectural wonders. I take a selfie outside with the Icelandic flag flapping in the wind, and my down parka hood pulled tightly around my head. This picture is today one of many on my writing room wall. I cherished the memory of my first day in this magical country.

Back at Hotel Cabin, I ask and am upgraded to an upper-level room with a double bed. The rooms are all very small and done in a contemporary style. I have a beautiful view of the bay and of snow-covered mountains in the distance. There are blackout curtains on the window to block the daylight, but I leave them open and nap in the sunlight.

After breakfast the next morning, Anna and Lars pick up the group for a long day touring the Golden Circle. Anna begins telling us about Iceland. The water from the glaciers, the central heating systems for everyone that comes from Geothermal energy, the heated streets in the city that keep the roads clear in icy conditions. We stop at a Geothermal plant and learn more. Iceland is the only country in the world to get 100% of its energy from renewable resources. Hot springs are harnessed for the steam to heat houses and the ever-popular swimming pool. Icelanders love to swim. And they love to sit in hot springs.

And now Anna tells us something else Icelanders love. Horses. Tiny horses. The excitement level on the bus gets to a giddy level when she says she has arranged a surprise for us. We will be stopping at a stable to see the world-famous Icelandic ponies! But she warns us, "Don't call them ponies. It is insulting because they are horses, not ponies."

The stable trip was an unexpected highlight despite all of the scenery we were taking in. Dozens of shaggy-maned horses were corralled outside. Everyone oohed and aahed. Inside we were seated around a riding ring where we were given a demonstration on different gaits, including one where the rider held a glass of water and didn't spill a drop. We learned that the breed was brought to the country by Norse settlers. They are hardy stock and can carry the weight of two men, and they have adapted to the climate. Due to restrictions protecting the breed, horses are not allowed to return to the country if they are shipped out. They are fiercely protected.

After the lesson, we enter the stable and have the chance to pet the friendly beauties. We all admired their beautiful manes and shaggy "bangs," The horses seemed to love the attention as if they knew they were adorable. We took turns taking pictures of each other with the little beauties. We reluctantly leave the stables and board our bus. That was awesome!

We ride on and on through the countryside seeing farms with fluffy sheep and lambs and, of course, horses. We arrive at our first waterfall Gullfoss. This is also our first encounter with paying for a toilet. Don't forget some change. We pooled our resources so we could all use the facilities. This is quite common in tourist areas in Iceland. There are a lot of stairs to descend to get a good view of the majestic and powerful waterfall. Some brave souls venture out on the cliff edges to get that perfect photo. I play it safe and stay on the walkways. Anna offers to snap my picture with the waterfall behind me. There is an opportunity for shopping here, and I take my first look at sweaters. Unlike Bali, Iceland is very pricey. Anna tells me the Icelandic sheep wool can take getting wet and still keep you warm, and I have been eyeing her beautiful sweaters over the past two days. I decide no, I will surely find one cheaper than in this tourist shop.

We stop for lunch and Geysir viewing. Geysir is the first documented geyser in history, and the name stuck. I get the opportunity to witness it erupting three times before I go back to the rest area, where we will be on our own for lunch. There are several restaurants and cafés to choose from. I get a delicious bowl of hot soup and bread with creamy butter. Butter and cream are of the finest quality here, along with the water.

We arrive next at the Continental Divide, where the tectonic plates meet. We walk along a path, and at one point, I have been on the North American side and then the Eurasian side. This is a historical place for many reasons, as the area Pingvellir was a sort of tribal meeting place where many events in Icelandic history took place. Also, *Game of Thrones* had done some filming here, which everyone was excited about. My second *Game of Thrones* location.

I can't tell you much about the ride back to Reykjavik because I fell deeply asleep and only awakened when we arrived back at the hotel. That was a lot of adventure for one day. I ate dinner at the hotel and slept like a log, even with the sun shining in.

The next morning, Anna and Lars picked us up and reminded everyone that they should have their bathing suits. Guess where we were headed today? The famous Blue Lagoon geothermal spa and hot springs. one of the 25 wonders of the world. It is fairly close to the airport, so travelers on layovers often take a shuttle to the spa to take in the waters. This was a to-do on everyone's list and a must-do for any visit to Iceland.

The walkway entering the spa and lagoon is lined on both sides with volcanic rock. In the modern entry, we are led through turnstiles and given robes, flip-flops and a towel. These cost extra unless you have them included in your tour, and believe me, you will want that robe! The changing rooms are vast and filled with lockers and showers. Once changed, I stood looking out the glass door at the lagoon beyond. It takes some amount of courage to step out into freezing temperatures in a bathing suit.

I braved it and hung up my robe and towel, and put my cell phone in the robe pocket. Sometimes you have to trust people, and in this case, it was ok. I entered the lagoon via a ramp, and the first thing you notice is, yes, it is indeed very warm. And the bottom of the lagoon is soft white silica mud and feels squishy to your feet. The farther you venture, the warmer you get. There is a bar where you can get some of the mud they use for the spa's products, and I slathered my face like everyone else. So there I am in the middle of Iceland in my bathing suit with my face covered in a white mud mask. Of course, I had to retrieve my phone, so I could take a selfie. Our group would be staying here for several hours, so I sloshed around until my body was prunelike. After a nice shower, I got dressed and entered Lava, the resort restaurant and had a bowl of soup and a martini of Icelandic vodka. I browsed the shop and looked over the very pricey creams and balms, and bought a small variety gift bag. All in all, it was a surreal experience. Back on the bus, Anna told us that just in case anyone had picked up a few of the black lava rocks as souvenirs, it was bad luck to take them out of Iceland. I was glad I didn't pick any up, although I was tempted.

I had not signed up for the next day's group tour because I wanted some time on my own to explore Reykjavik. That morning as I exited the hotel, I found that the wind was so strong I could barely walk. I pulled out my street map and started by heading to the bay and the waterfront walkway. I stopped at the Concert Hall for a brief respite inside the lobby before venturing out again. I followed my map and went to the main shopping district Laugavegur. I smelled something wonderful. A tiny crêpe shop with delicious aromas wafting out the open door. I sat and ordered a savory breakfast crêpe and a big mug of hot chocolate. Heaven.

Back outside, I could see the spire of the church a few blocks away. I started walking in that direction. I would take in that breathtaking view Anna had described that first day. Little did I know that the observation tower is not glassed in. When I ascended by elevator and stairs, the freezing wind howled through the open stone windows. I am very afraid of heights. But I steeled myself. Anna was indeed correct about the view being spectacular. I took some amazing photos of the city and the harbor below.

I walked the streets of the shopping district, browsing the stores looking at those beautiful sweaters, but still, my budget told me no. No sweater for you today. I walked on and on in the general direction of my hotel. In the late afternoon, I stopped at a burger place that I had read about having excellent lamb burgers. I needed to sample some local cuisine, and they had a view of the very famous site of the Summit between President Reagan and Mikhail Gorbachev. An unimposing white building that resembles a farmhouse with a view of the bay. And the lamb burger didn't disappoint, although I wouldn't want my daughters to know I ate a little lamb.

Walking back to the hotel, I found a small market a block from my hotel, and I bought some items from the deli-type case. And next door to that was a wine shop where I purchased a bottle of wine. Needless to say, I was going to spend the rest of the now evening inside. Once again, my blackout drapes remained open. I witnessed a semi-sunset over the bay and about two hours of not quite darkness every night. And the room stayed quite warm due to the thermal heating. I was content with British telly and my goodies.

My last day. I would explore more of Reykjavik and maybe get that sweater. When I left the hotel, I discovered that I had only thought it was windy the day before. It actually almost knocked me down. I went back inside and had a taxi called. I rode to the History Museum and spent some time enjoying the exhibits and artifacts. It was hard to step back out into the wind, but I braved it and followed, much like in Sevilla, the spire of the church as a guidepost and arrived back in Laugavegur shopping district. My stomach was starting to rumble, and I spotted the Old Iceland Restaurant. I took a seat by the window so I could watch the passing foot traffic. I was the only diner in the place. I ordered a feast of shellfish soup, filet of cod with garlic mashed potatoes, carrots and parsnips. The cod was the best I have ever eaten. Fresh and delicate. It was one of the most memorable meals I have been lucky to savor.

The walk back to the hotel was treacherous because I was walking against the brutally strong wind. Holding onto signposts and railings wherever I could to keep from getting knocked down. It worsened the closer I got to the bayfront. I did make it back without injury, but I will tell you the next day, my arms, shoulders and legs felt like I had done a very strenuous workout. I called it my wind walking workout.

Something I need to mention about the Icelandic people, they are extremely superstitious. They believe in hidden people or elves that live within the lava rocks. This land of modern technology, glass buildings and geothermal, nuclear plants has quite the culture built around elves. Do you believe in elves?

And about that sweater. I broke down last minute and bought one at the duty-free shop at the airport minutes before boarding my flight home. And I will never regret that purchase.

Gratitude Message:

I am grateful for all my Facebook friends who told me to say YES to Iceland. Many had been there or knew people who had been and loved it. Land of Fire and Ice, where I felt the energy of Mother Earth coursing through my entire body from feet upward. The beautiful surreal scenery, the charming people, the magnificent, proud horses. To the top of the cathedral facing my fear of heights, to see the breathtaking view of the city below. I give thanks and gratitude for this experience.

"A good beginning makes a good ending." —Icelandic Proverb

CHAPTER FIVE – ITALY

"I love places that have an incredible history. I love the Italian way of life. I love the food. I love the people. I love the attitudes of Italians." —Sir Elton John

I decided to go Old World this trip when Groupon Getaways offered a 9-day Venice, Florence & Rome by rail trip. Pasta and pizza and the Vatican sounded wonderful. My flight would go through JFK to Frankfurt to Venice. It was a very long trip, and Frankfurt airport is massive. I was exhausted by the time I reached the boarding gate to Venice. I actually was telling myself this could be my last trip. As I sat at the gate, I was joined by a Nun and some Italian school girls. Soon a German pilot sat near me. He was talking on his cell phone in German, and when he ended his call, the Nun started speaking to him in Italian. Another passenger approached him and asked him about the flight in English. Those conversations reminded me that throughout the world, many people speak multiple languages. I felt like I was lax with my high school Spanish, and I wondered if it was too late in life to start to learn other languages. Something I am still working on.

After arriving at the Venice airport, which is on the mainland, I joined a group at the shuttle desk. We followed a guide outside to a boat terminal. We boarded a beautiful small wooden speedboat with our luggage piled in front. We sped across the harbor and entered the canals of Venice. Everything is about the water in Venice, a city literally built on the water. Passing boats carried washers and dryers being delivered, mail, crates of fruits and vegetables and tourists. I was dropped at my Hotel Tre Archi, named for the bridge next to it. There are approximately 400 bridges in Venice, and mine was beautiful.

I was exhausted and hungry, but my room was not yet ready. I sat in the lobby trying not to doze off when the bartender came in carrying a pizza. I asked him where he got it, and his response was, "Very Good Pizza." Ok, it must be very good but where? He took me outside and pointed two doors down the sidewalk. It actually was called Very Good Pizza. At that moment, I gazed at the canal, at the Tre Archi bridge and the boats and water taxis, and I told myself to wake up and be present in Venice. I went to

Very Good Pizza and ordered by pointing at the menu. A funghi and prosciutto pizza. It came in one size. And I sat looking out at the canal and ate every bite. The best pizza of my life. Very Good.

My hotel room was beautiful. Flocked green and gold wallpaper. And over the bed, a green and gold Murano glass chandelier. The hotel had many Murano chandeliers, and the one in the lobby was magnificent. Red and purple and gold. I ate my breakfast of Rice Krispies with banana and strong coffee the next morning under that chandelier.

I was signed up for the included walking tour and boat trip to Murano that first morning. I was to meet the group at the Santa Lucia train station. The map seemed pretty straightforward, but the twists and turns of Venice are deceptive. Also, I should mention there are no cars at all here. Boats, bicycles and feet are the modes of transportation. There are water "buses" and water taxis, but according to the map, I should be ok walking. I came to a dead-end and was trying to get my bearings when a middle-aged couple came to the same dead-end. We recognized each other from breakfast, and we decided to team up to find the train station. So began a great friendship with Carol and Tony from Cincinnati. We found the train station and our guide for the day, Maria. She was a school teacher from Venice. But she explained no one can afford to live in Venice except on the mainland, and most of the people who work there take the train in and out every day.

We boarded a boat and wound through the canals. The water was not very high that day, and Maria explained the metal planks that are raised in the doorways to keep the water out when it did rise. She said that mold is, of course, an issue in the lower-level apartments and shops. We passed houses and buildings with small docking areas. Ancient rings attached to ancient buildings for mooring boats. We set off across the bay for Murano. Maria pointed out an island that she explained was the cemetery. There are not many spaces available anymore, and it is very expensive. Versace is buried there, and Sir Elton John has a space, or so she told us.

Murano is a quaint village that is home to the world-famous glass factories. We started with a demonstration, and it was incredible. Watching the artisan create before our eyes a stallion on its hind legs, its front legs kicking the air. Then he made a vase using several rods of colored glass that he heated in a fire oven. All done the traditional way. Each piece of art is handmade. Such a treat to experience.

After the demonstration, we entered the showroom. Overhead in every room were magnificent chandeliers, each one unique. Statues and vases and jewelry. I bought a few bracelets and a small vase. I longed for one of those chandeliers, but that was not in my budget. And no, unlike the Icelandic sweater, I would not be picking one up at the airport!

Arriving back in Venice, we started our walking tour. Maria showed us interesting landmarks, and we followed her through alleyways and crossed bridges stopping to photograph the colorful gondolas as they glided along the canal. Listening to the echoes of the gondoliers singing. We passed many shops selling Venetian masks, and Maria spoke of Carnival. A time when Venice is overrun by tourists and the Venetians leave the city. We emerged at St. Marks Square. The cathedral with its beautiful carvings and the golden dome of the Basilica, the Bell and Clock and the ramp walkways. These are everywhere in the square to keep tourists' feet dry when the water is high. So far, my feet were dry, but then I purposely took my waterproof hiking boots, having done my research.

Maria bade us farewell and left us on our own. My new pals Carol and Tony were going on another tour, so we parted ways. I strolled the square and bought some mask magnets and some other trinkets. I found a high-class hotel and sat in the outdoor restaurant, and had lunch watching the gondolas and the cruise ships in the distance. My waiter had the shiniest patent leather shoes, and I giggled as he reminded me of a character from the movie *The Birdcage* as he maneuvered on the terrace tiles.

He gave me directions on my map for my next destination, my gondola ride. I joined several other tourists on board, and we glided down the Grand Canal and through the alleyways waving to people on the bridges we crossed under. Everyone has to take a gondola ride while in Venice. I took the water bus back to Tre Archi and ate a marvelous pasta dinner at a restaurant next to the hotel that Carol and Tony recommended. A splendid day in Venice.

The next morning was departure day for
Florence. When I looked out the front of the
hotel, the water was up to the door. A bell
was ringing, and the desk clerk explained it
was the high water warning and that no
water taxis or buses were running. Uh Oh. I
could not drag my suitcase to the train
station with the water so high. I asked the
clerk for advice, and she said that you could
hire a private boat. Luckily, Carol and Tony
came into the lobby, and we decided to
share a ride. We made it to the train station,
and Carol and I wandered the shops while
Tony happily watched our luggage.

The train ride to Florence was wonderful.
Trains in Europe are comfortable
commuters' dreams. The scenery whizzed
by, and we quickly arrived in Florence. My
friends and I shared a taxi to our next hotel.
This hotel was modern and efficient, the
Grand Hotel Mediterraneo. With a first-class
restaurant, enormous breakfast buffet and a
large lobby bar. I ordered pasta and wine at

the lobby bar, and since it was St. Patrick's Day back home, I had the green pesto pasta. I went to see David at the Accademia Gallery, which was extremely crowded, and I walked back to the hotel.

After the wonderful breakfast buffet, I decided not to join the group tour. I wanted time for myself. I let Carol know to tell the guide not to worry about me. It was lightly raining and a little chilly as I walked to the Uffizi Gallery. The line was very long, and I asked a guard which line was the ticket line and which line was the line for entering if you had a ticket. He politely asked me if I was alone, and when I nodded yes, he took my arm and led me around the line and let me enter the ticket office. Another perk of solo travel? I would say yes. The Uffizi is like a treasure chest of master artworks. I marveled at the Roman sculptures and the tilework. I had been honored to see a DaVinci exhibit at the North Carolina Museum of Art, but Uffizi's collection is astonishing. Works by Michelangelo and Raphael were beautiful. My favorite was Botticelli's Birth of Venus. I was very glad I decided to forgo the walking tour and take in the Uffizi.

Outside I visited a leather shop and was custom fitted for an Italian leather jacket that would be shipped to me. My treasure from the trip. I had some pizza at a sidewalk café, and since the rain was increasing, I walked back to the hotel arriving just as a downpour started. I rested and read in my room for a bit until the sun burst out, and I could see across the river up on the hill the park that I had read held another David. I took a taxi up the steep hill passing beautiful villas with views of the Arno River. My taxi driver waited while I captured the stunning views of the city below with my camera. I would say my tour of Florence, a city so beautiful, was complete.

I arrived in Rome the next day. The Hotel Villafranca was an older hotel, and I would hear some guests complaining about mold in the bathrooms. Not me. I asked for an upgrade and was told to take the elevator to the third floor and take a left, and straight ahead, I would see a white door with no room number. I had an actual brass key, not an electronic card key. My room was "the Bridal Suite"! Not very modern, but I had a large sitting room, a kitchenette, a huge bathroom (no mold) and a canopied bed. The view was not spectacular, just the alleyway behind the hotel and the backs of the adjoining hotels and cafés.

Our group Roman tour guide AnnaRita had left a note to meet her in the bar in one hour. I joined others for some nice red wine that AnnaRita had ordered. She handed out maps of the city and asked who had added the Vatican and Colosseum tour the next day. I was signed up, as were Carol and Tony. Those who hadn't opted for the tour asked to join, but AnnaRita said she had no extra tickets as it was approaching Holy

Week and the Vatican would be crowded. I was glad I had added this when I booked my Groupon. Just like a trip to Venice not being complete without a gondola ride, my visit to Rome had to include the Vatican and Colosseum.

My friends and I left the hotel together and strolled the streets until we found a nice café that had walls lined with wine bottles. I had the absolute best Carbonara ever. When in Italy, don't shy away from carbs. You will walk them off anyway! I would eat in this same café again, sampling an Alfredo. And wine.

The next morning was a cool drizzling rain, and the trip to the Vatican required a hair-raising taxi ride through the city. Ancient ruins next to modern office buildings and typical big city traffic sum up what I saw.

Outside the Vatican was a mob scene of international tourists and a tank and soldiers protecting the mecca. Tour guides held up colorful flags to keep their groups together. AnnaRita had our red and gold flag waving in the air, and we entered the queue to get inside. Heavy security was present, and everything went through the x-ray machines and scanners. To say you could hardly move was an understatement it was so crowded. Once we started our tour, it was a bit less crowded, but you had to keep moving and stay with the group.

The Vatican, if you don't know, is actually a city within the city of Rome. The Pope has a residence within the walls, and according to AnnaRita, the current Pope prefers a more modest living style and resides in the house but without many of the opulent furnishings. I was able to get a photo of the house through one of the Museum windows. First, though, we entered Saint Peter's Basilica, where once again I felt the presence of Spirit within the holy place. The massive number of tourists kept hushed voices in reverence.

I wandered through, taking in the ornate baptismal fountain and viewing the many Chapels that open off of the main church. It is the largest church in the world, and I am in awe, as are all the other souls among me. Enormous statues of Saints dwarf the viewers. Saint Peter, one of the favored disciples, is purported to be buried here. The sheer size of this place is overwhelming. I see AnnaRita's flag waving at the entrance, which seems miles away. It is time to move on.

Our group enters the Gallery of Tapestries, a seemingly never-ending hallway with rich, heavy tapestries hanging from the walls, ornate tile floors and frescoed ceilings are framed in gold. It was from one of the windows in the Gallery that AnnaRita whispered to me and pointed to the home of the Pope, and I snapped a picture. The crowds in groups led by their guides and flags did not push or hurry. Everyone stopped to take it all in.

From the Gallery, we wound around and entered the ultimate destination for most of the tour groups. The Sistine Chapel. The Suisse Guards spoke in English, "No Pictures!" "No Cell Phones!" This was not a casual request. The Chapel is small in comparison to St. Peter's, but it is the most beautiful of all. Before we entered, AnnaRita told us Michelangelo's reluctance to take the commission of painting the ceiling of the Chapel. Pope Julius II was persistent, and the artist could not say no. It is said, according to AnnaRita, that the Pope is depicted in the Last Judgment painting as revenge. The ceiling is nothing short of a wonder. The creation of Adam is the perhaps most famous part of this magnificent work, but the total scope of the work is nothing short of breathtaking. Few people spoke. Some wept. Some had mouths hanging open. A few pulled out cells only to put them back upon the harsh look of the guards. I sat on a bench and took it in as best

I could, trying to sear it into my memory forever. And I did. Because it is that important and beautiful.

We emerged into St. Peter's Square, and AnnaRita pointed out the famous balcony where the Pope would wave to the onlookers below. Hundreds of folding chairs were set up for the upcoming services of Holy Week. What it must be like to be among the faithful having the experience of being in attendance.

Then we shopped. Everything or nearly everything in the gift shop is blessed by the Pope. I don't imagine each individual rosary is blessed, but en masse, maybe? I purchased some beautiful Murano glass rosaries for family members even though we are not Catholic. But they were beautiful and blessed by the Pope. I purchased many plastic rosaries for fellow workers who are most certainly Catholic and trust me, they were so happy and grateful when they got them and saw the little card saying "Blessed By The Pope."

It was starting to rain quite heavily and had grown quite cold when we arrived at the Colosseum. We took a rather out-of-place modern glass elevator up to the top and viewed the interior. It is pretty cool to see it in real life. AnnaRita talked about where patrons would sit. Of course, the Emperor and Senators had the best seats. Knights, dignitaries and the rich had the next best seats. The highest level, as we would call the nosebleed section, was for the poor, slaves and women.

After completing our tour, I joined two sisters who were in the group, and we decided it was too cold and too wet to do anymore but to return to our hotel, so we grabbed a taxi. I didn't even go to my room since the Vatican Gift Shop was delivering my packages. Carol and Tony were drinking wine at the bar, and I joined them. We walked next door and ordered some pizza and returned to the bar and spent the evening in Italy eating, drinking wine and laughing. They were departing early the next morning, so we said our goodbyes and exchanged email addresses.

On my last day in Italy, I was signed up for the Street Food Tour with AnnaRita. Her usual note was under my door the next morning instructing me to meet at the Fountain of the Four Rivers at Navona Square. It was not raining and only a little chilly when I arrived. Only the two sisters and one other of the group were joining us. The fountain itself contains an Egyptian obelisk and is surrounded by the four major rivers of the four continents, the Nile, the Danube, the Ganges and the Rio de la Plata.

We entered a coffee shop in the square, and AnnaRita ordered us coffees. The scene was chaotic, with people ordering coffee and sweets at the bar. Thank you, AnnaRita! We entered an outdoor marketplace full of pastas, cheeses, fruits and flowers. AnnaRita brought us a feast from vendors that we ate sitting around a fountain. Next, we wound through the streets and alleys, and we came to a bakery shop where we were treated to Arancini, Rice balls stuffed with cheese and deep-fried. We passed an area of shops that were Versace, Pucci, Prada and Armani until we got to a little café where we sat outside and ate the most amazing fried artichokes and plates of bruschetta. AnnaRita hugged us and said, "Ciao!"

Everyone was stuffed, but we decided to take in one last sight: The Trevi Fountain. We got our bearings and set off with our maps. After a few wrong turns, we found it. We squeezed in together and took photos tossing our coins over our shoulders. What a great Tour of Italy!

That evening, I went back to the little café and had my last dish of authentic Italian pasta and a glass of red wine. Not only had I experienced Italy, but I had also made some friends.

Gratitude Message:

I am grateful for pasta, pizza, vino, history, art and religion. For the sights, sounds and tastes of Italy. The canals, gondolas and beautiful masks of Venice. The art and serenity of Florence. The history and monuments of Rome. A true trip of a lifetime for so many people. I can close my eyes and meditate on the ceiling of the Sistine Chapel and the sheer beauty of Michelangelo's craft. And pizza will never be the same.

I give thanks for this experience.

"Mary had been raised in a family where blood was as thick as tomato sauce." —Lisa Scottoline Rosato & DiNunzio

CHAPTER SIX – AFRICA

"Lions aren't used to other creatures staring them down. It's a good tactic for life too: even if you're terrified inside, stare it in the eye." —Boyd Varty

L et me start out by telling you that my African Adventure was not a Groupon Getaway trip. Groupon does offer African safaris, but my trip was not one of those. This is a completely different trip from any others I have taken. I applied and was accepted to a Life Coaching experience with a very famous Life Coach. This was an expensive endeavor, but there was a payment plan, and I saved for nearly a year for this trip. I am not going into too much detail about the Life Coaching part because that is too personal, and I also don't want to write about my fellow students. Suffice it to say, it was the experience of a lifetime, and we all keep in touch and support one another in making our dreams turn into realities.

I left from Atlanta and got my upgrade to first class on Delta One, and let me tell you, that is posh stuff. I had what I call a cocoon and was pampered from takeoff to landing. I really liked that cocoon, and it made the seventeen-hour flight to Johannesburg much more comfortable. Plus, the food and wine were pretty darn tasty.

I had booked one night at the Intercontinental Hotel at the airport to make things easier. The room was gorgeous and comfortable, and I was tired and ordered room service. I watched mostly British television and slept soundly.

The next morning was easy since I was already at the airport. A van took me to a smaller airfield with a garden and waiting area, where I met some of my fellow students. We boarded a tiny, very tiny airplane and flew off to our home away from home, the Londolozi Game Preserve. Londolozi is a truly magical place. Owned by the Varty family for decades, it started as a hunting safari camp, but the Varty brothers had an epiphany of sorts and became conservationists. The once-barren land that was mostly void of wildlife started a rebirth. Lions and, most notably, leopards started to return. It grew lush and alive. The tents were replaced with beautiful modern camps. Visitors came from around the world to take game drives in Land Rovers and photograph the abundant game. The wild animals became unafraid of the humans riding in the tin cans. Not to confuse you because they aren't tame; they are still wild, but since no one is shooting at them, other than with cameras and cell phones, they pretty much ignore the tourists.

We landed at the small airstrip and were greeted by our Ranger guides. I had been assigned to the group that was with Ranger Shaun and Tracker Jerry. I would be with them twice a day for five days on a morning and evening game drive. I had an unfortunate accident the day before I left home, having badly sprained my ankle. To say I was taken great care of is an understatement. The staff provided me with my own wooden box to climb into the Rover, and I got to sit up front next to Shaun for most of the rides. Jerry had a perch seat on the front of the vehicle so he could watch for tracks and signs. We arrived at Tree

Camp, where we would be meeting our Coaches and spending our time in our cottages and eating our meals together.

My cottage was gorgeous, and yes, everything sort of hangs above the trees and the savannah below. A living room, bedroom with a fluffy white bed enclosed in mosquito netting and a huge bathroom with a soaking tub looking out to a walled garden, everything perfect. A deck and small round pool were off the back. Multiple latches on all the doors inside and out are there to keep the monkeys from entering your room and stealing your possessions. We were warned when we left our cottages to be sure to secure all the latches!

After seeing our cottages, we gathered in the main lounge and deck at Tree Camp. The tables had been put together to form a square so we could all see each other. Our coaches were waiting for us. Boyd Varty and his sister Bronwyn Varty-Laburn were two of our coaches. What an incredible experience. Boyd is one of the very best storytellers I have ever heard, and you should check out his Ted Talks, podcasts and read his books.

We had lunch and did some Life Coaching, during which a herd of giraffes passed the deck. We were told to get our coats and prepare for our first game drive. We would be out for about three hours, and the sun would set, and it would become chilly. Part of our experience was that all of our game drives were to be silent. This turned out to heighten our experience because when you are silent, all of your other senses take over. You notice things. Shaun and Jerry used hand signals and whistled to indicate tracks and signs. It wasn't long before we saw a herd of elephants. A large bull and several others, including a couple of babies, were grazing on some trees. Magnificent massive creatures only a few feet away. No one was allowed to bring cameras or cell phones on that first drive, so we used our eyes instead of looking through a lens. That evening we saw many impala and giraffes. The only sound we made were gasps, and all of us had smiles plastered on our faces. Shaun got a radio call and made a gesture that we would come to know as a leopard track. His fist pointed down, and then his fingers making dot signs on his forearm. We headed toward the airstrip, stopping once to see the setting sun blazing over the savannah.

As we passed the airstrip, we could see the lights of the other Rover coming toward us. Shaun pointed to something coming down the road between the vehicles. It was a lone leopard! It passed inches from my seat in the open Rover! This was just our first outing. What would the subsequent game drives bring? When we arrived back at camp, Shaun and Jerry smiled at me and said that the leopard was very close to me. I was shaking with both excitement and fear, but at that moment, I realized I was safe with them, and they would not put me or any of the others in danger. They know the animals, and they have the skills to handle the situation.

We entered the boma, which is a walled outdoor area filled with lanterns and a big fire pit. Dinner every night was served here, and I tried boar and springbok and oxtail soup and other native dishes during my stay, and everything was delicious. Londolozi is, after all, a five-star resort.

Mornings would begin with a bang on the door and a cheerful Good Morning! If you didn't answer, the banging kept up. When you did answer, you were greeted by a cheerful staff member with a tray of coffee and a biscotti. This was roughly 5:30 AM, and we had 30 minutes to meet at the camp driveway to board our Rovers for our morning drive. Hot water bottles and blankets were in our seats. Our first-morning drive began with the sunrise. We crossed the bridge heading toward the airstrip and stopped to view several hippos crawling from the banks into the lagoon. Today we were allowed our cameras and phones, but we remained silent.

The radio chattered, and Shaun whispered into it. He signaled Jerry, who left his perch seat and joined the passengers in the back. Soon we joined the other vehicle with our fellow students and sat quietly watching a female lion lying in the grass. Shaun gestured at his chest, and we all saw the blood on the lioness's chest from her nighttime kill. Suddenly a large male lion ambled toward her. She ignored him, and then another male appeared at a slight distance away. Competition. The lioness rose and appeared to be listening to something far away. She started off into the brush.

Shaun followed her, and this was my first time driving through brush and thorns and low-lying branches. It was really exciting and made me feel like an adventurer, which I actually was. Shaun pointed and stopped the Rover. Here we were in the midst of a pride. The lioness we had been tracking joined her sisters. Five or six large females and about eight cubs. Can I just tell you that was the thrill of a lifetime? We sat silently for about an hour watching them. They already ate an Impala for breakfast, and one of the cubs was possessively protecting a leg. Don't be squeamish, as this is life. Real life.

The pride rose together, and the cubs followed the females to find their place to sleep in private. I got one of the very best pictures I have ever taken of a mother licking her cub clean from their breakfast. We pulled back out on a dirt track, and in an open spot, Shaun and Jerry served us tea and biscuits. Our group was all ladies, and Shaun indicated a safe spot behind a bush for us to take a bathroom break.

Every morning and every evening, we took these drives. We saw everything you could want to see. Elephants at dusk, a rhino with a calf at a watering hole, giraffes eating leaves from high branches, another lion pride dozing in the sun with a male sleeping stretched out on his back. One day we saw endangered and rare wild painted dogs napping under a copse of trees. Shaun whispered how lucky we were to witness this group. Wild dogs are returning to Londolozi to hunt and to give birth to their pups.

On the second day, we stopped and parked next to some other vehicles and walked through the trees, where we were greeted with a picnic lunch and a bathroom tent. We had a cookout and did some coaching sitting under the trees with full china and silver. Our guides and trackers joined us, and we had a marvelous time.

Another day we stopped and left our vehicles, and it was the first time I really noticed the rifle on the front of the Rover. Shaun took it out of its case and told us to follow him and Jerry. We went down a steep hill, and two of my companions took my arms and helped me on my injured ankle to navigate down. We came to the Sand River bed, which was dry this time of year, and we joined a circle sitting in the river bed, and our guides held their rifles and kept a watch to keep us safe. Boyd began telling the story of Londolozi and his family. It was a moment I will never forget. His beautiful hushed voice sharing this wonderful tale of adventure and conservation and rebirth.

I didn't have much downtime at camp, but I did get a massage between coaching and game drives. The Healing House is located at Varty Camp down a path from Tree Camp. It overlooks the Sand River and provides, naturally, first-class spa services. I was so relaxed I almost missed lunch that day. I also toured the Village with Bronwyn, who is a wonderful inspiration. The staff lives in the village, and everything is very ecofriendly. There is a school for the staff children and lots of classes for adults as well, The Good Works Foundation is part of Londolozi, and they do amazing charitable work throughout South Africa.

On our last night, we were treated to the usual feast but with lots of entertainment. Boyd told some hilarious stories of guests and nature, including a baboon in the suite of a Saudi Prince that had booked the entire resort. The Londolozi Ladies Choir sang to us, and some of the trackers did a traditional Shangaan dance. We joined in and had a very fun evening.

Our last day was a bit sad as we gathered for breakfast, and our suitcases were brought from our rooms and stored outside the lounge for our departing flights. We gathered for a group photo which I have framed in my writing room. A few of our group departed on a flight to Cape Town. The rest of us rode together to the airstrip with one younger member of our group given the trackers seat. Departure was bittersweet, but I was able to hug Shaun and Jerry goodbye and get a picture with them.

I arrived back in Johannesburg feeling an empty space in my heart. Londolozi had touched my heart and soul, and I vowed to return someday. After a night back at the Intercontinental, avoiding television, I boarded my 17-hour flight back to the states. In my upgraded cocoon.

Gratitude Message:

I am grateful to have been introduced to Londolozi Game Reserve and the conservation of the Varty Family by one of my mentors Martha Beck. I was blessed to see this incredible place of true nature, beauty and sanctuary. The staff of Londolozi with their true joy and comradery. I am grateful to my fellow students for sharing this time and their stories and for their life-long friendships. The "real world" truly is Londolozi, and I know I will return.

I give thanks for this experience.

"I never knew of a morning in Africa when I woke up that I was not happy." —Ernest Hemingway

CHAPTER SEVEN – POSTCARDS

"We travel because we need to because distance and difference are the secret tonic of creativity." —J. Lehrer

I have traveled the world alone. From the classics like Spain and Italy to the exotic islands of Bali and Iceland. On an African Safari of self-discovery. No matter where I have been, all of my journeys have taken me to the same place over and over. A place within myself where I discovered a person I really didn't know existed. ME! Spending time alone or with tour groups helped me come out of my shell and learn to rely on my own brave heart, my own two feet and my instincts. It has opened my body, mind and spirit to the wonders of the world around me. Seeing sights, I never imagined. Hearing my own true voice. Tasting foods I would never have tried before. Meeting people of different cultures and religions. Stepping out of my personal comfort zone. Living my best life and realizing a lifelong dream of travel.

When you travel alone, there are so many perks. You eat when you are hungry, and you sleep when you are tired. Your agenda is set by you and you alone. So many times, I have been in the silence of a cathedral or just wandering a street, and I witness tourist couples whining or arguing with each other about what to do next or how they want to go in different directions. I hear children complaining they are bored or tired. I just laugh and ask myself, "Ok, where to next? Yes, that little café looks perfect for a coffee or a glass of wine and a short rest. The museum? Sounds perfect. Maybe back to the hotel to read or watch some foreign television for two hours?" I never get an argument. And if you wonder what is on tv in Bali, it is classic American westerns! BBC is popular everywhere in the world. I watched *Big Bang Theory* in Italian. I don't mean to imply I waste precious time on television, but when I rest, I switch it on to get the full cultural experience.

I have learned a great deal about what I enjoy and things I skip if I just don't feel like it. Just do the things you want and see as much as possible because you may never get another chance to see The Sistine Chapel or Icelandic horses. Take it all in and take some nice pictures. But don't forget to look up from your camera or phone and really

SEE and imprint that sight in your memory. Make a postcard memory to cherish forever.

Thank you for joining me on my travels and listening to my stories of my experiences. Now go look for a trip that you always wanted to take or one that you never expected to take and get to know yourself!

CHAPTER EIGHT – TIPS

"An investment in travel is an investment in yourself." —Matthew Karsten

- Always ask for the upgrade. You won't get it if you don't ask.
- Leave the hotel after check-in unless it's very late at night. Even if you just walk around the block, you will

immediately immerse yourself in the country you are visiting.

- Always leave yourself one or two days with no tours just to wander by yourself. Some of my best days have been solo wandering days.
- Pack light. Obviously, if you are going to Iceland, you will need some layers but keep your packing simple. I have definitely overpacked before and found I didn't wear everything I packed.
- Invest in good walking shoes or hiking boots, and make sure you bring Band-aids!
- Invest in a good camera. There are many small ones that still will give you excellent quality photos. I have a Canon G9-X. I can download my pics in the hotel in the evening and post them on social media. My friends are always happy to see where I have been.

- EAT THE FOOD! Try something local. It doesn't have to be terribly exotic but trust me, you will enjoy almost everything, including barbeque springbok!
- If you are on a train or tour bus, look out the window. Don't study a map or read a book. Take in the scenery.
- Talk to the locals. Chat with the waitstaff, the hotel clerk, the taxi driver, the shopkeeper. Ask questions and soak up the local color.
- Visit churches, cathedrals, mosques and other places of worship. You will see the pinnacle of architecture, artifacts and artwork inside these magnificent spaces.
- Most importantly, spend time getting to know yourself. Really enjoy your alone time and be free to be you!

Bon Voyage! Yours truly. GG

PS My next adventure will be a cruise to Croatia and Greece. The ship departs from Venice, and I hope I can stop by and have a slice of Very Good Pizza!
PPS Sadly, that trip was canceled due to the Covid-19 virus, but I will get there eventually!
PP PS I am booked early next year for a cruise on the Nile!

"To travel is to live." —Hans Christian Anderson

"Twenty years from now, you will be more disappointed in the things you didn't do than by the ones you did do." —Mark Twain

AUTHOR BIO

GG Rush is a perpetual student and seeker of knowledge, experience and enlightenment. She is a "Wayfinder Life Coach In-Training." She attended "Martha Beck's African Star Program" at Londolozi Game Reserve in South Africa. She is certified Reiki II and is studying Reiki III under Master Marina Lando MS, who has also taught her Aromatherapy, Chakra Balancing, Toxic Emotions and the ancient art of Pulse Reading. She has traveled the world solo and will continue her journey to see the world and find herself. GG, aka Gail Rush Gould, resides in Cary, North Carolina, with her cat Bella.